■ AT HOME

CLEANING UP

HOW TRASH BECOMES TREASURE

EVE & ALBERT STWERTKA
PICTURES BY MENA DOLOBOWSKY

JULIAN Ⓜ MESSNER

The authors are grateful for the hospitality and expertise generously offered by representatives of:

The Department of Waste Management, Materials Recovery Facility, and Landfill, the Town of Brookhaven, N.Y.

The Solid Waste Department, the Town of North Hempstead, N.Y.

The Department of Sanitation of the City of New York.

Omni Technical Services, Uniondale, N.Y.

Design by Malle N. Whitaker.
Manufactured in the United States of America.

Lib. ed.
10 9 8 7 6 5 4 3 2 1
Paper ed.
10 9 8 7 6 5 4 3 2 1

Library of Congress Cataloging-in-Publication Data
Stwertka, Eve.
    Cleaning up / Eve and Albert Stwertka; pictures by Mena Dolobowsky.
        p. cm.— (At home with science)
    Includes index.
    Summary: Discusses the problem of trash and what can be done with it, including the partial solution of recycling.
    1. Refuse and refuse disposal— Juvenile literature. 2. Recycling (Waste, etc.)—Juvenile literature. [1. Refuse and refuse disposal. 2. Recycling (Waste)] I. Stwertka, Albert. II. Dolobowsky, Mena, ill. III Title. IV Series.
    TD792.S84   1993 91-28777
    363.72'8—dc20   CIP AC
    ISBN 0-671-69461-8 (lib. bdg.)
    ISBN 0-671-69467-7 (pbk)

Books in the **At Home with Science** series by Eve and Albert Stwertka

A Chilling Story: How Things Cool Down

Drip Drop: Water's Journey

Heat, Lights, and Action: How Electricity Works

Hello! Hello!: A Look Inside the Telephone

Tuning In: The Sounds of the Radio

Cleaning Up: How Trash Becomes Treasure

CONTENTS

THE TRASH INVASION

Do you want to get rid of a worn out pair of sneakers? Or a plateful of chicken bones? Or a torn mattress? What a relief to know that a sanitation truck will come around soon to pick up the things you and your neighbors want to throw away!

But wait a minute! Picking up the trash is only part of the job. The other part is finding a place to put it down.

Trash and garbage—or **solid waste,** as it is sometimes called—can't be put down just anywhere. You probably know some of the reasons: It looks ugly and smells bad. It attracts animals such as rats and mice, and insects such as flies and roaches. It provides places where germs can breed and make you sick. If you set it on fire, the smoke dirties the air.

Throughout history people have tried different ways to dispose of their trash. They would bury it, burn it, throw it into the river, or toss it over a cliff. Often they just let it pile up in a heap.

Each of these methods caused some pollution. But as long as there were few people and plenty of empty space, the environment did not suffer too much from this trash.

7

Today, though, the earth is chock full of people. We use more products, containers, boxes and wrappers than our ancestors. We throw out far more waste.

Tough new materials called plastics were not invented until the twentieth century. Today we use them and throw them away with great ease. But most plastics don't break down or fall apart as other materials do. They can lie in the sun, or in the ground, or under water, without changing. They will take up space for hundreds of years.

8

In recent times, more and more waste has been thrown out of homes, stores, offices, and restaurants. Many communities have run out of disposal places. Garbage dumps threaten to pollute the groundwater, nature's deep-down storage pools that supply many areas with pure drinking water. Garbage burned in badly-made incinerators can dirty the air with black smoke. And trash dumped in waterways tends to clog rivers, lakes, and oceans.

Many areas of the country are passing laws against dumping and burning garbage.

Communities that can't dispose of their own solid waste now pay high prices to ship it to less populated areas. And sometimes the people in those areas grumble and threaten to send it right back again. It's not surprising, then, that someone actually suggested packing the world's trash into rockets and shooting it off to the moon!

SORTING THINGS OUT

Every day we collect thousands of tons of trash. But safe places to put it have become scarce and expensive. To reduce the bulk of the **waste stream,** we sort out some of the valuable contents and sell them to be **recycled,** or used again. Recycling has another advantage. It saves precious raw materials and energy.

In some communities the sanitation department is in charge of recycling. In others, though, the people who live in the community do some of the job themselves. They return soda cans and bottles to the store and collect the deposit that was paid on them. They separate used aluminum, tin, or steel cans, aluminum foil, glass jars, and plastic containers from their other refuse. These *mixed* **recyclables** are then picked up by the sanitation department of the town. Many communities also ask people to save newspapers, magazines, and cardboard boxes and tie them in bundles for recycling.

Once a week or so, trucks bring recyclables and newspapers to one central place. This is the **Materials Recycling Facility** or MRF. The people who work there sometimes call it the "Merf." An open area along one side is the tipping hall. Here, the trucks enter and tip out their load. Vehicles that look like small snowplows push the mixed recyclables onto a moving conveyor. While the stream of trash is carried into the building, another conveyor brings the newspapers to a machine that ties them into gigantic bundles.

Put on your hard hat and step inside this vast and noisy place. Overhead you will see conveyor belts moving the mixed materials through a series of sorting stations that tower in the air. Some workers have to climb up steep metal stairs to get to their jobs.

Some communities pre-sort their recyclables before they get to the MRF, but many others do not. What comes to the MRF usually looks like a topsy-turvy mixture of things. Rapidly, though, each sorting station now separates one material from the rest, and sends it away in a different direction.

First, a large magnet pulls off steel cans and other objects containing iron. They drop through a chute into a **compactor** on the floor below. This powerful machine squeezes them together, then forces them out in solid blocks that weigh about 1400 pounds.

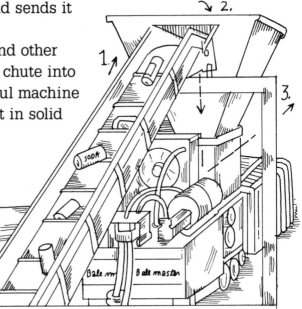

1. CANS TRAVEL UP CONVEYOR.
2. NEXT, THEY ARE DROPPED INTO A CHUTE.
3. AT LAST THEY ARE COMPACTED.

CANS GOING UP CONVEYOR TO BE COMPACTED.

Keep a list of everything your family throws away during one week. Then check off all the items that can probably be recycled.

We throw away enough soda cans to keep an entire recycling plant in business!

SODA CANS ✓
CHICKEN BONES ✓
BOTTLES ✓
CARDBOARD BOXES ✓
DIAPERS

ALUMINUM CANS AND STEEL CANS ARE COMPACTED SEPARATELY.

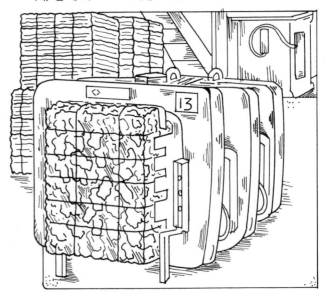

A COMPACTOR PUSHING OUT COMPACTED CANS.

GLASS SORTER

Aluminum is harder to separate because it is not attracted by ordinary magnets. A special magnetic system is needed for the job. It creates small electric currents in the scraps of aluminum, which make them jump off the conveyor belt. The scraps drop through a chute into another compacting machine.

Now glass and plastic refuse fall on a series of **shaking tables** with openings in the bottom. Small glass pieces fall through. They are not usable because their colors are all mixed together. Workers sort the larger glass pieces by the most common colors—clear, green, and brown. The new glass made from them will keep those colors. The pieces then drop into noisy crushing machines, and are carted away in bins.

SHAKING TABLE

15

Now only plastics remain on the belt. They move to a sorting table. Workers stand on both sides, wearing gloves and face masks. These protect them from cuts and chemicals, and from breathing fumes of leftover food and laundry products.

Sorters can tell the difference between seven kinds of recyclable plastic. With both hands they quickly pick out the pieces riding by, and place them in different bins. Like the metals, plastics drop through chutes into powerful compactors. A **baling machine** ties up each type of plastic with wire, forming bales that can't come apart.

You, too, can recognize different kinds of recyclable plastic. Look at a variety of plastic containers and bottles. Make sure the caps are screwed on tight, then turn them over carefully. Notice the recycling symbol, code letters, and number on the bottom. The two most commonly used plastics are **PETE** (polyethylene terephthalate), called Type 1, and **HDPE** (high-density polyethylene), called Type 2. These are recycled into new bottles, tubing, pails, toys, and many other things. PETE can also be turned into fiberfill for winter jackets and sleeping bags.

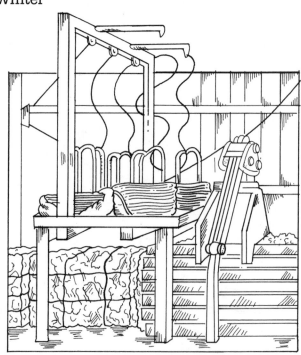

PLASTICS ON CONVEYOR

PLASTIC SORTERS

BALING MACHINE

16

Meanwhile, the newspapers have been neatly compacted and tied by their own baling machines. On the ground, below the conveyors, there are stacks of different kinds of bales all around. They are made of glittering aluminum, dull-looking steel, brightly-colored plastics, or gray and white newspaper. They are too big and heavy for one person to carry. Even a bale of plastic soda bottles weighs about 800 pounds.

A worker in a forklift truck picks up the bales and takes them to open gates along one side of the building. Here, they will be loaded into trailer trucks.

When the trucks are full, the drivers take off to many different factories. The trash that nobody wanted has become raw material for many new products.

WORKER IN FORK LIFT
TRUCK PICKING UP BALES.

BALES BEING LOADED ONTO
TRAILER TRUCKS.

FROM DUMP TO LANDFILL

Years ago, garbage, junk, trash, harmful chemicals, and medical wastes all ended up, helter-skelter, in the town dump. This was usually a deep pit somewhere in the countryside, where people threw anything—from a dead skunk to a broken bicycle.

Dumps attracted wild animals, rats, and flies. Now and then, the sanitation department would set the dump on fire. This would burn down some of the bulk and destroy pests and germs. But smoke from the smoldering garbage hung in the air, and the woods sometimes caught fire accidentally.

19

TRUCKS LINED UP AT THE DUMP.

A LAYER OF SOIL IS NOW SPREAD OVER A NEW LAYER OF TRASH.

Later, as towns grew, the dumps also expanded. But nobody wanted to live near them. This made people begin to realize that waste had to be disposed of more scientifically.

Experts in waste management advised that each new layer of trash be topped with a layer of soil. Many towns set aside separate disposal sites for harmful chemicals, such as cleaning fluids and pesticides. Often, trees were planted around the dump to hide it from sight and to purify the air.

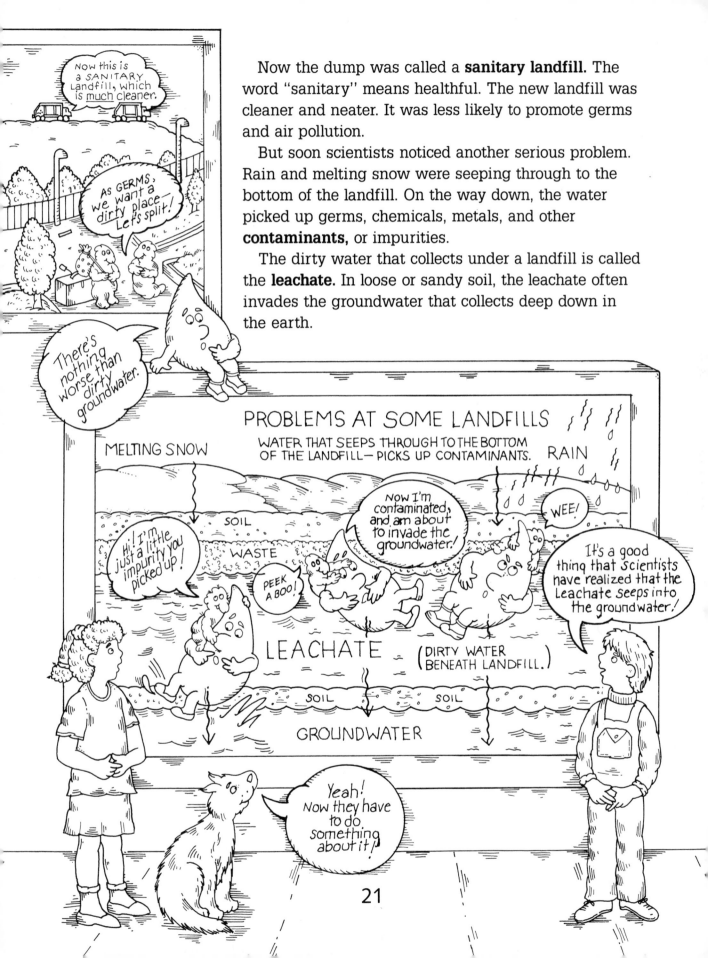

Now the dump was called a **sanitary landfill**. The word "sanitary" means healthful. The new landfill was cleaner and neater. It was less likely to promote germs and air pollution.

But soon scientists noticed another serious problem. Rain and melting snow were seeping through to the bottom of the landfill. On the way down, the water picked up germs, chemicals, metals, and other **contaminants,** or impurities.

The dirty water that collects under a landfill is called the **leachate.** In loose or sandy soil, the leachate often invades the groundwater that collects deep down in the earth.

21

Today a landfill is built in a way that will prevent this. First, engineers make sure that the pit to be used is huge—many acres across and at least 20 feet deep. Then, it is lined with thick waterproof clay soil. Where clay is not available, a double layer of strong plastic is put down instead. This acts as a well, and leachate collects here. Next, a system of pipes is installed to drain this polluted liquid. Every day, tank trucks pump out hundreds of gallons of waste water and take it away to a sewage treatment plant. There it is cleaned and released again into a river, lake, or ocean.

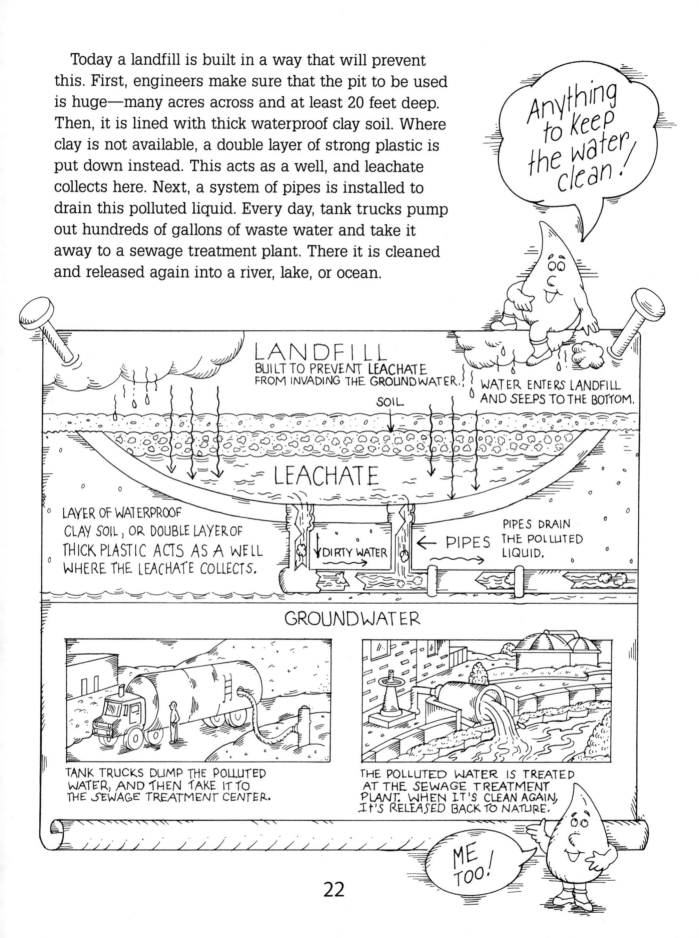

Anything to keep the water clean!

LANDFILL
BUILT TO PREVENT LEACHATE FROM INVADING THE GROUNDWATER.

WATER ENTERS LANDFILL AND SEEPS TO THE BOTTOM.

SOIL

LEACHATE

LAYER OF WATERPROOF CLAY SOIL, OR DOUBLE LAYER OF THICK PLASTIC ACTS AS A WELL WHERE THE LEACHATE COLLECTS.

DIRTY WATER

← PIPES

PIPES DRAIN THE POLLUTED LIQUID.

GROUNDWATER

TANK TRUCKS DUMP THE POLLUTED WATER, AND THEN TAKE IT TO THE SEWAGE TREATMENT CENTER.

THE POLLUTED WATER IS TREATED AT THE SEWAGE TREATMENT PLANT. WHEN IT'S CLEAN AGAIN, IT'S RELEASED BACK TO NATURE.

ME TOO!

22

After some years, the landfill grows into a hill, and then into a mountain. From the top, you can see far into the countryside. Trucks drive up the slope and tip out their load.

What a mixture of things tumbles out of those trucks! Sofas and stoves, eggshells and orange peels, cameras and refrigerators. Often, swarms of screeching birds swoop down to snatch a meal.

23

As soon as a fresh load of trash is on the ground, bulldozers come in, push it around, tear and break down any large pieces, and spread everything flat. Heavy trucks with spiked steel wheels come roaring up. They drive back and forth over the trash to compact it. Then, a dump truck empties out a huge load of soil or sand to cover it.

BULLDOZERS BREAK TRASH APART.

SPIKED STEEL-WHEELED TRUCKS COMPACT THE TRASH.

DUMP TRUCKS SPREAD SOIL OVER THE TRASH.

Make a model landfill in a tall glass jar. Put three inches of sand in the bottom. Then line the entire jar with two layers of strong plastic. Now "tip" in your garbage—a few vegetable and fruit peels and a broken eggshell. Don't use meat or bones. Pour in a 1/4 cup of water; this will act like rain. Cover your landfill with an inch of sand. Put the lid on lightly; don't screw it on tight.

Your landfill will ferment and rot. But if the liner is strong enough, the sand at the bottom will remain un-polluted and dry. Gases will form. You'll be able to smell them.

MAKE YOUR OWN LANDFILL

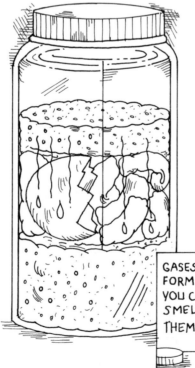

1. Put three inches of sand in the bottom of a large jar.
2. Line the entire jar with two layers of strong plastic.
3. Tip your garbage with a few vegetable and fruit peels, and a broken eggshell.
4. Pour in 1/4 cup of water.
5. Cover with one inch of sand.
6. Put the lid on lightly.

GASES FORM. YOU CAN SMELL THEM.

24

The shredded trash now starts to decompose among the layers of soil. **Decay bacteria**, or germs, help this material decay. These tiny organisms digest waste matter and break it down, so that eventually the refuse becomes just soil again. In the process, a gas called **methane** is formed. It smells very bad, but makes a good fuel.

At a modern landfill you can see pipes coming out of the sides of the pit. They tap the methane and lead it out to a generator that burns the methane gas for fuel. The generator makes electricity, which is usually used by the local community.

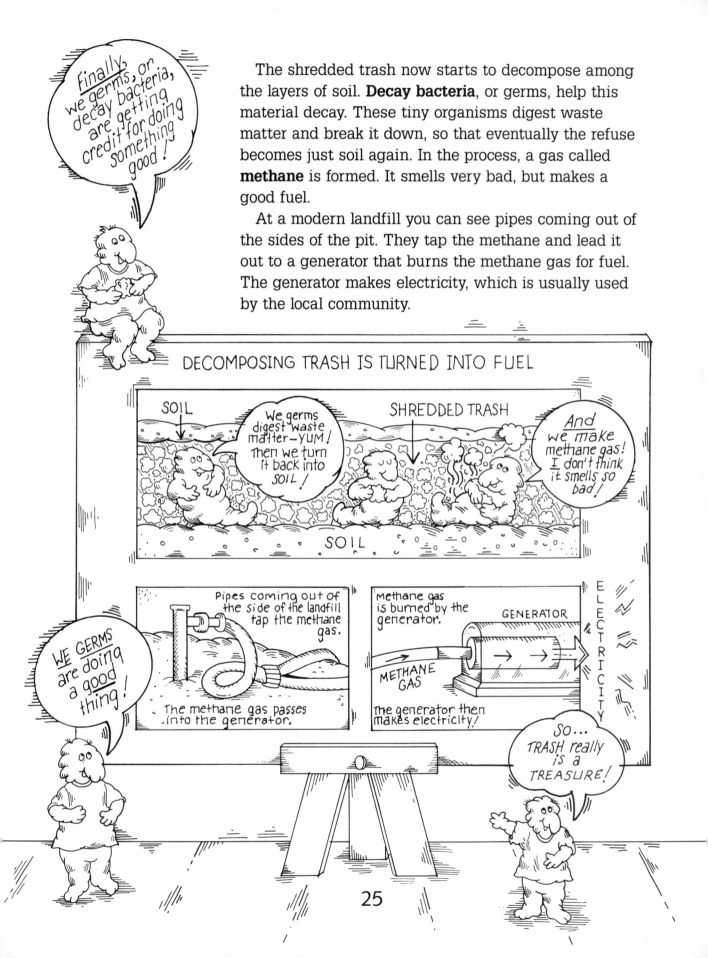

When the landfill has grown hundreds of feet high, it becomes too steep for trucks to climb. Now it is covered with a final layer of soil and seeded with grass. It is left alone to stabilize, or settle down. After a few years, shrubs and wildflowers begin to grow. Birds make themselves at home.

A mountain now exists where the land was once flat. Perhaps it will be turned into a park, a sheep meadow, or a ski slope. But long before that, space for a new waste-disposal site must be found.

LANDFILL GETTING FINAL LAYER OF SOIL.

SAME "LANDFILL" SOME TIME LATER!

FIRE AND ASHES

A landfill needs large empty tracts of countryside. In places where land is scarce and expensive, communities have often tried to dispose of their waste by burning it. It seems like an easy solution. Fire reduces large and bulky objects to a small heap of ashes. It also destroys disease-causing germs. Unfortunately, though, experts have discovered that burning or incinerating garbage can cause many problems.

Before people were concerned about polluting the environment, incinerators that could burn large quantities of trash began to appear on the outskirts of many cities. The black smoke pouring from their chimneys could be seen for miles around.

Soon, many apartment houses installed small incinerators of their own. People would throw all their refuse down a chute into the cellar. Whatever fell down there was burned in the incinerator. As a result, black, greasy soot was released in the middle of cities. The soot flew into apartment-house windows. It blackened the curtains and the furniture.

Even worse were the invisible gases that escaped. All garbage contains large amounts of plastics. When plastics are burned, the original materials are destroyed, and new materials form. One of these is a gas called dioxin. Dioxin is a poison that is suspected of causing cancer.

Garbage also contains metal cans. The high heat inside the incinerator causes many metals to form new materials, some of which are poisons. These poisons attach themselves to the dust and ash that go up the smokestack.

After this was discovered, laws were passed forcing the inefficient, old incinerators to be shut down.

Recently, scientists have developed "clean" incineration systems. They are equipped with **scrubbers** that filter out polluting dust particles from the gases that go up the smokestack.

These huge, complicated incinerators do much more than reduce waste to ashes. They are designed to be **resource recovery plants** that convert thousands of tons of garbage into an energy "resource." Instead of burning valuable coal or oil, they burn garbage to run the generators that make electric power.

One of the simplest modern incinerators uses the so-called **mass burn process**. Cranes dump the entire waste stream directly into a single furnace. Large quantities of air are forced into the furnace to make sure that burning takes place at very high heat. The higher the temperature the more likely it is to destroy some of the dangerous gases, such as dioxin, that are formed during burning. The heat produced by the burning garbage boils water in enormous tanks to make steam. Sometimes the steam is used directly to heat buildings and operate machinery. More often, though, the steam runs a generator to produce electricity.

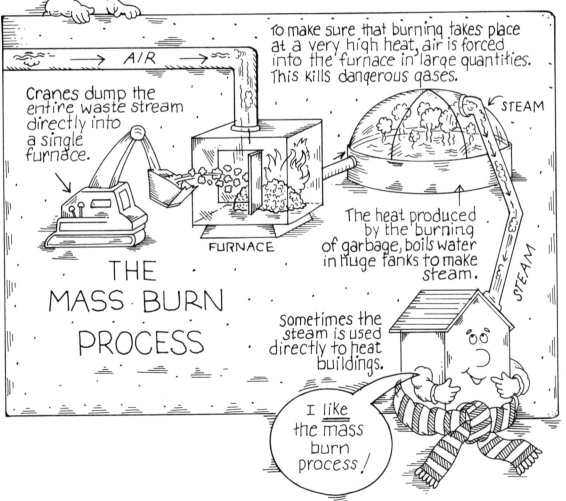

31

A second important type of incinerating plant devotes itself to recycling as well as the production of fuel. It is known as a **refuse-derived fuel** facility, or RDF.

In an RDF plant, all metal is removed from the trash by large magnets. A conveyor belt then carries the remaining trash through a series of filters. These screen out such materials as glass and dirt, and anything else that won't burn. The metal and glass are sold to scrap dealers for recycling.

The remaining trash passes through a machine that shreds everything into small pieces. This material is the RDF. It is often compacted into small pellets and sold to power plants, where it is burned, along with coal, to make electricity.

All incinerators leave deposits of ashes and other unburnable materials that must be carted to a landfill.

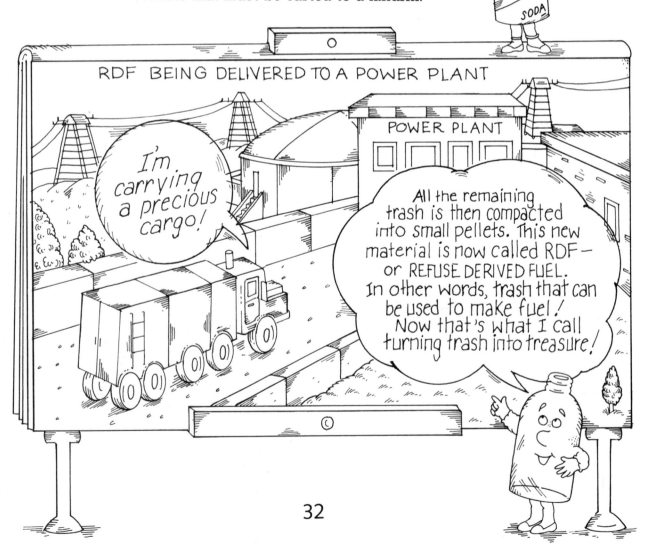

In spite of the protective devices in modern incinerators, some scientists still think that scrubbers prevent harmful particles from escaping into the air. What happens, though, is that the particles remain in the ashes instead. The cleaner the air, the more contaminated the ashes. To keep the groundwater safe, incinerator ashes are best disposed of in special landfills for hazardous wastes. Here the wastes are covered and surrounded with clay or concrete to isolate them from the environment.

TRASH INTO TREASURE

Did you ever think that garbage would make a fascinating subject of study? The things people throw out tell us a lot about their way of life—their diet, clothing, furnishings, and forms of entertainment. In fact, **archaeologists**—the scientists who study how humans lived long ago—get much of their information from the refuse people left behind.

We tend to look down on the very idea of trash. But experts in waste management know its value. Even before recycling, solid waste can yield precious items. Expensive tools, antiques, jewelry, and money are often found in it. In one California recycling plant, workers recovered $20,000 in coins in just six months' time. This did not include the paper money and checks people threw out by accident.

Sometimes trash is in demand just for its bulk. It can be piled up to form an artificial mountain and used to help create more land. This garbage, or landfill, is often used to fill in wet or swampy ground. For instance, the shoreline of lower Manhattan was extended with landfill. New York actually gained an extra quarter of a mile of land all around to use for new buildings and parks.

When something in your house seems ready for the trash pile, take a good look at it first. You may be able to rescue it. Perhaps you can fix it, trade it for something else, give it away, or find a brand new use for it. To everyone's surprise, it could turn out that you have discovered a treasure.

GLOSSARY

Archaeologist (ar-kee-OL-uh-jist) Someone who studies the customs of people who lived long ago.

Bale A large, tightly-packed bundle.

Baling machine A machine that makes bales and ties them with wire.

Compactor (KOM-pack-tur) A machine that presses materials into tight bundles.

Contaminant Any substance that pollutes air, water or soil.

Conveyor belt (kun-VAY-ur belt) An endless band, traveling on rollers, used to transport things across short distances.

Decay bacteria (di-KAY bak-TEER-ee-uh) Tiny organisms that cause garbage to decompose.

Decompose (dee-kum-POZ) To rot or fall apart in decay.

Generator (Jen-ur-ay-tur) A machine that uses steam or other forms of energy to produce electricity.

HDPE High-Density Polyethylene. A heavy plastic, called Type 2, used to make detergent bottles, pails, hoses, and other products.

Incinerator (in-SIN-ur-ay-tur) A furnace for burning solid waste.

Leachate (LEE-chayt) Polluted liquid that forms at the bottom of landfills.

Mass-burn process A way of burning solid waste to produce useful energy.

Materials Recycling Facility MRF. Sometimes pronounced "MERF."

Methane A burnable gas formed by decomposing garbage.

Mixed recyclables (mixt ree-SY-klu bulz) A combination of reusable materials, such as glass, plastic, and metals.

PETE Polyethylene Terephthalate. A lightweight plastic, called Type 1, used to make soft-drink bottles, fabrics, and other things.

Recycling (ree-SY-kling) Treating waste materials so they become raw material again.

Refuse-Derived Fuel RDF. Burnable pellets made from shredded waste.

Resource recovery plants (REE-sawrse ree KUV-ry) Places where usable materials are sorted out from solid waste.

Sanitary Free of dirt, designed to prevent disease caused by germs.

Sanitary landfill A scientifically planned waste disposal site where pollution will be prevented.

Scrubbers Filters to clean the air that comes out of incinerator smokestacks.

Shaking table A screening device that lets small pieces of material drop through the bottom.

Solid waste All trash and refuse that is not liquid.

Waste management The work connected with safe, clean and economical trash disposable.

Waste stream The endless supply of waste products that must be disposed of.

Waste-to-energy A way to burn garbage as a fuel to make steam for heating or generating electricity.

39

INDEX